Parent's Prayers

A PECU Pocket Book

Parent's Prayers
A Pecu Pocket Book

ISBN: 978-1-949289-25-1
Copyright © 2025 Peculiar Productions, LLC

Peculiar Productions
PO Box 1441, Madison, AL 35758
www.pecuproductions.com

All rights reserved. No portion of this book may be reproduced, stored in a retrieval system, or transmitted in any form or by any means - electronic, mechanical, photocopy, recording, or any other - without the PRIOR written permission of the copyright owner – except for brief quotations in critical reviews or articles.

All Scriptures are from the KJV translation unless otherwise stated.

Parent Prayers for Our Children

My children are not my responsibility. That may be a weird statement to share at the beginning of a book focused on prayers for our children, but it's something I accepted early on as a parent – forgot in the middle of being a parent – and somehow, I have managed to find my way back to that truth.

We are all God's children. Even the ones that I raised are His.

So, even saying they are MY children takes on a quality of possession I'm trying to fight. Because I am the steward of those lives. God placed them in my path for a particular reason, and I want to be a good and faithful steward over those lives and for those lives.

When the children were younger, we made particular choices for them. We chose to homeschool. We chose to eat meals as a family. We chose to limit sodas. We chose to read at night and during naps. We chose to play games as a family. We chose to be outside.

Because, as the stewards of those young lives, it was our job to make choices.

As they grew older and more aware, we encouraged them in the choices they made. Because, as a good and faithful steward, a HUGE part of my job is to train them up in the way they should go ... and then to allow them to go in that Way.

And now that they are adults, my job has shifted yet again. I have less influence on them than at any other time in their lives. I've leaned into the power of prayer.

Because if you have a parent (or a grandparent) who is invested in praying for your life, then you might as well give in to that because that parent isn't going to shut up.

Or that's what I heard from a comedian one day, and I'm using that to drive my daily prayer life for the children.

I started keeping my first prayer journal many years ago. Like a lot of things, I've let it slide during seasons. But when I start back up, it's always the same:

Date a page,
Write out your prayer in "thanksgiving" format – giving thanks and praise for what has happened even before it is fulfilled,
Date the prayer (and notate request),
Speak the prayer aloud.

I add to my prayer journal any prayer requests I get directly (and I try to get specific outcome desires so we pray in agreement). I add those prayers that stir me awake in the middle of the night. I add those prayers coming from encounters during my day.

Although all of my prayers are mixed together, I've pulled out a few that focused specifically on the children.

I've left the name open so you can fill in the prayer with the names of your children.

There are also places for you to create your prayers or to add notes recording the results of your prayers.

Feel free to reach out to me if you ever want someone who will agree with you in a specific prayer for the children.

Parent's Prayer

For a Stronger Walk

Lord, thank You that daily You are growing [name] to a stronger walk in You. Thank You that [he/she] is encountering You in a personal way, so faith roots are deep and the foundation built with those roots is unshakable. Amen.

Everyone who hears these words of Mine and puts them into practice is like a wise man who built his house on the rock. – Matthew 7:24

Date:

For a Straight Path

Lord, help [name] choose to look to You in all the ways that [he/she] may go. Help [him/her] embrace the truth that with You and in You, the paths are made smooth. Help [name] to see that a walk in You is departed from evil. Help [name] understand that health and strong bones come when we depart from the path of evil.

Lord, guide [name] to the place where [he/she] will put [his/her] trust in You and You alone by strengthening a personal relationship with You. Amen.

Trust in the Lord with all your heart and lean not on your own understanding; in all your ways submit to Him, and he will make your paths straight. – Proverbs 3:5-6

Date:

Parent's Prayer

Growth for the Parent

Lord, grow in me Your Love so that I show unconditional love to [name] in ways that [name] will receive.

Lord, create a pathway of God Love and God acceptance in [name]'s life so that [name] begins to pour that God Love back out. Amen.

Be completely humble and gentle; be patient, bearing with one another in love. Make every effort to keep the unity of the Spirit through the bond of peace. – Ephesians 4:2-3

Date:

Love All In

Lord, help [name] today to love you wholeheartedly, to be all-in with You. Let [him/her] be so full of You that there is no room for anything else.

Lord, thank you that You are helping the focus of [name] be always You. Let [his/her] eyes and ears be always good, positive, encouraging, and uplifting so [he/she] sets a firm foundation for standing in You. Amen.

Let the words of my mouth and the meditation of my heart be exceptional in your sight, O Lord, by Rock, my strength, and my Redeemer. – Psalm 19:14

Date:

Parent's Prayer

Opening Doors

Lord, thank You for opening the doors for new friendships for [name]. Friendships that will help [him/her] and encourage [him/her] into living [his/her] life for You and in You.

Thank You that You are drawing [name] towards the hearts that will fuel [him/her] with Your joy and Your laughter. Amen.

Two are better than one; because they have a good reward for their labor. For if they fall, the one will lift up his fellow. – Ecclesiastes 4:9-10

Date:

Empowered to Parent

Lord, I know that in You alone can I be the parent You have called me to be. Each morning, let me choose to focus on You. Through a God focus, let me walk out my day in a Light that shows my children Your Way. Amen.

I have no greater joy than to hear that my children walk in truth – 3 John 4

Date:

Parent's Prayer

Unique Identity

Lord, thank you that [name] has a unique identity in You. Help [name] to daily see You, and to follow You with a joyful heart. Open [name]'s eyes so that Your vision becomes [his/her] vision for [his/her] life. Amen.

Who hath saved us, and called us with a holy calling, not according to our works, but according to His own purpose and grace, which was given us in Christ Jesus before the world began. – 2 Timothy 1:9

Date:

Speaking Truth

Lord, thank You that You are teaching [name] to speak Your truth over [his/her] life so that [name] is not snared by the words of [his/her] mouth. Let Your words of hope and joy be [his/her] default. Amen.

Whoso keeps his mouth and his tongue keeps his soul from troubles. – Proverbs 21:23

Date:

Parent's Prayer

Being a Light

Lord, let Your Light so shine in me that [name] will see and I don't have to tell. Help me to walk this Light in a way that shows [name] Your path. Amen.

Help me be the good and faithful steward over the life of [name] who you have placed in my hands.

Lord, daily grow my Faith to live in Your promises and be an example of You.

You are the light of the world. A town built on a hill cannot be hidden. Neither do people light a lamp and put it under a bowl. Instead, they put it on a stand, and it gives light to everyone in the house. In the same way, let your light shine before others, that they may see your good deeds and glorify your Father in heaven. – Matthew 5:14-16

Date:

A Good Steward

Lord, I know that I am Your steward over [name]. I know that [name] is Yours. Teach me to speak Your words in [name]'s life and over [his/her] life. Let my focus always be You first to quieten the world. Amen.

Let no corrupt communication proceed out of your mouth, but that which is good to the use of edifying, that it may minister grace unto the hearers. – Ephesians 4:29

Date:

Parent's Prayer

A Family of Believers

Lord, help [find the family of believers who will continue to feed [his/her] heart so that [name] continues to grow into all You have called [him/her] to be.

Help [name] connect with people who will help [him/her] understand and dwell in Your complete love.

Let [name] experience You and Your Word in a personal way through the relationships around [him/her]. Amen.

Wherefore, comfort yourselves together, and edify one another, even as also ye do. – 1 Thessalonians 5:11

Date:

Promises of Protection

Lord, thank You for Your promises of protection. Help [name] find [his/her] ways into the shadow of the protection of Your wings.

Thank You, than in You no weapon formed against [name] may prosper when [he/she/ chooses to reside in your protection.

Help me be an example and encouragement that points to that place of Your safety. Amen.

He who dwells in the secret place of the Most High shall abide under the shadow of the Almighty. – Psalm 91:1

Date:

Parent's Prayer

Hedge of Protection

Lord, thank You for putting a hedge of protection around d[name]. Thank you for nudging [name] to put on the full armor of God:
Helmet of protection
Breastplate of righteousness
Belt of truth,
Boots of the gospel of peace

Thank you that [name] takes up the sword of the spirit, and leans all in with You, to hold tight to the shield of faith so [name] will stand boldly in you. Amen.

Put on the whole armor of God, that you may be able to stand against the wiles of the devil. – Ephesians 6:11

Date:

Increasing in Knowledge

Lord, thank You for daily increasing the heart and mind of [name] in the knowledge of You. Thank You for feeding [him/her] more of You and for surrounding [him/her] with relationships that fuel more of You.

Let an ever-increasing desire for You stir in the heart of [name] until you become the driving force for every step.

May all of You color all of [name]. Amen.

That you might walk worthy of the Lord to all pleasing of Him, being fruitful in every good work, and increasing in the knowledge of God..
– Colossians 1:10

Date:

Parent's Prayer

Drawn to God

Lord, thank You that You are drawing [name] to a deep and personal relationship with You. May [name] be always learning, open to attaining more knowledge in You, and setting a firm foundation of Wisdom, so [name] can stand firmly in Your joy. Amen.

The fear of the Lord is the beginning of wisdom: and the knowledge of the holy is understanding.
– Proverbs 9:10

Date:

Peace Beyond Understanding

Lord, pour Your peace over [name]. May [name] stay focused on You and in You so the peace that passes all understanding deflects the anxiousness and worries of the world. Amen.

You will keep him in perfect peace, whose mind is stayed on You because he trusts in You. – Isaiah 26:3

Date:

Parent's Prayer

Clarity for a Parent

Lord, thank You for the revelation You are pouring over me for [name]. Thank You for Your clarity to see [his/her] heart. Thank You for Your wisdom to speak Love in, over, through, and for [his/her] life.. Amen.

If any of you lack wisdom, let him ask of God, that giveth to all men liberally, and upbraideth not; and it shall be given him. – James 1:5

Date:

Comfort for Today

Lord, thank You for pouring over [name] Your love and comfort today. Help [name] find [his/her] way to Your path for [his/her] life. Thank You that You are surrounding [name] with relationships that bring Your joy, peace, and comfort to [his/her] heart. Amen.

Wherefore comfort yourselves together, and edify one another, even as also you do. – 1 Thessalonians 5:11

Date:

Parent's Prayer

Delight in God

Lord, thank You that You have made [name] to delight in You. You sent Your son to save [name] so that [he/she] could have life and have it abundantly. Pour into [name] understanding that leaning into You will provide all [he/she] needs to stand. Amen.

The Lord your God in the midst of you is mighty; He will save, He will rejoice over you with joy; He will rest in His love, He will joy over you with singing. – Zephaniah 3:17

Date:

Strength of Joy

Lord, thank You that You have created us for a life of abundant joy in You. Grow [name] to lean into You today so that Your joy overflows [him/her] and becomes the strength on which [name] stands.

When joy is the strength on which [he/she] stands, then stress, worries, anxiety, and doubt have no place to attach or stand.

Thank You that You are daily helping [name] lock into the truth that You are the peace that passes all understanding. Amen.

Now the God of hope fill you with all joy and peace in believing, that you may abound in hope, through the power of the Holy Ghost. – Romans 15:13

Date:

Parent's Prayer

Made On Purpose

Lord, thank You for [name], who You have fearfully and wonderfully made. Help [name] come to know the individual You created, so much so that [name] can walk boldly in that uniqueness.

Thank You that [name] has been made for such a time as this. May the truth of Your design fill [name] with the strength to stand. Amen.

For we are His workmanship, created in Christ for good works, which God hath before ordained that we should walk in them. – Ephesians 2:10

Date:

Path to Joy

Lord, thank You that You are the only path to Joy. Help [name] build a life on Your Joy by being actively and personally invested in Your Word. Grow [name] daily to find gratitude and to allow the gracious spirit and focus to be the guide for each step. Amen.

You will show me the path of life; in Your presence is fullness of joy; at Your right hand there are pleasures for evermore. – Psalm 16:11

Date:

Parent's Prayer

Look for Joy

Lord, thank You for guiding [name] to a place of Joy in You. Thank You that [he/she] invests in seeing the truth of joy ... that joy is a choice founded in You.

Thank You that You are helping [name] look for Joy all around [him/her] so that [he/she] can find Your joy that becomes a solid foundation of strength on which [name] stands. Amen.

I will rejoice in the Lord. I will joy in the God of my salvation. The Lord God is my strength, and He will make my feet like hinds' feet and he will make me to walk upon my high places. – Habakkuk 3:18-19

Date:

The Steward Parent

Lord, thank You for giving me Your child, [name]. Thank You for calling me to be the steward over the life of your child. I know You have a plan and a purpose for [name]. Help me to pour into [his/her] life what is needed to build [name] up for Your purpose design.

Thank You for helping me today to be invested in my walk with You so that through my walk I will be an example and a help to [name]. Amen.

Live such good lives among others that, though they accuse you of doing wrong, they may see your good deeds and glorify God" – 1 Peter 2:12

Date:

Parent's Prayer

Growing Fruit

Lord, thank You for Your fruit growing in [name]'s life. Let today bring a better Spiritual understanding of Your will for [his/her] life so [he/she] grows bolder in walking out each step of Your design.

Thank You for Your Spirit in [name]'s life. Let the relationship growing up from a focus on You continually be the guiding force in [his/her] life. Amen.

I am the vine, you are the branches: He that abides in me, and I in him, the same brings forth much fruit: for without Me you can do nothing. – John 15:5

Date:

Growing in God

Lord, thank You that [name] is growing in Your law so that [he/she] loves Your law. Thank You that when [name] walks in You nothing can make [him/her] stumble. Amen.

This book of the law shall not depart out of your mouth; but you shall meditate on it day and night, so that you may observe to do according to all that is written therein. For then, through this focus, you will make your way prosperous, and you will have good success. – from Joshua 1:8

Date:

Parent's Prayer

For Peace

Lord, thank You for Your provision, peace, and wisdom that is engulfing [name] today. Let [name] see clearly and step with bold intention in obedience to Your directions. Amen.

The Lord bless you, and keep you. The Lord make his face shine upon you, and be gracious to you. The lord lift up His countenance upon you, and give you peace. – Numbers 6:24-26

Date:

Next Step Accuracy

Lord, thank You for Your crystal clear clarity and pinpoint accuracy for the next step [name] needs to take. Let [him/her] have eyes to see and ears to hear. Amen.

I will instruct you and teach you in the way which you shall go: I will guide you with My Eye. – Psalm 32:8

Date:

Parent's Prayer

Relationships of Joy

Lord, thank You for pouring over [name] Your love and comfort today. Help [him/her] find [his/her] way to Your path for [him/her]. Thank You for surrounding [name] with relationships that bring [him/her] Your joy and peace. Amen.

God comforts us in our tribulations so that we can comfort others who are in any trouble through the same comfort that we have been comforted by God. - from 2 Corinthians 1:4

Date:

Leaning Into God

Lord, thank You that today is a day of rejoicing for [name]. Thank You that [he/she] is leaning into Your truth for [his/her] life with such determination and focus that nothing can hold [name] back from Your Abundant Life. Amen.

If you continue in My (Jesus) word, then you are my disciples indeed; and You shall know the truth and the truth shall make you free. John 8:31-32

Date:

Parent's Prayer

The Power of Prayer

Your children are not your responsibility. This can't be said enough. You are called to be stewards in their lives and for their lives.

Prayer is your job.

The results are God's.

When we make prayer for the children a priority for our day, then we set a foundation for their walk and grow ours.

The supplications and prayers of a righteous man (walking with God) will accomplish many things. (from James 5:16).

May these prayers be the beginning of bold, purposeful, and specific prayers to help spark the abundant life for you and your family.

To continue building an arsenal of prayer, email us contact@pecuproductions.com and we will send you the *Praying Scripture download* – our gift to you.

www.ingramcontent.com/pod-product-compliance
Lightning Source LLC
Chambersburg PA
CBHW052127070526
44586CB00016B/2127